BALLET TECHNIQUE

This statuette, which shows Mme. Karsavina in the first act of Giselle, was made by Seraphim Soudbinine in Paris, 1910. It was executed in biscuit porcelain by the Imperial Factory of Porcelain in St Petersburg.

TAMARA KARSAVINA

BALLET TECHNIQUE

A Series of Practical Essays

BY

TAMARA KARSAVINA

WITH A FOREWORD BY
DAME MARGOT FONTEYN, D.B.E.
AND 27 ILLUSTRATIONS

THEATRE ARTS BOOKS
NEW YORK

COPYRIGHT © 1956 BY TAMARA KARSAVINA

FIRST PUBLISHED 1956

REPRINTED . . . 1957

REPRINTED . . . 1970, 1973 and 1976

THEATRE ARTS BOOKS

333 SIXTH AVENUE, NEW YORK NY 10014

Library of Congress Catalog
Card Number 68–28084

PRINTED IN GREAT BRITAIN

FOREWORD
by MARGOT FONTEYN, D.B.E.

MADAME TAMARA KARSAVINA is a most rare artist. She is still a most rare artist although it is many years since her retirement from the stage.

During the Diaghileff era, a period of great artistic advancement in ballet, she was at her height. With her particular dramatic qualities allied to a fine ballet technique, she was more than a great ballerina of the classical tradition; she was also the perfect inspiration and foil to the choreographic genius of Michael Fokine.

That she so well fulfilled his demands of dramatic expression we know because we hear and speak not of "Karsavina the Ballerina," but of "Karsavina as Giselle," or "as Columbine" or "as The Firebird." It is evident that she became completely identified with each rôle she danced.

In this book it is fascinating to learn how she must have made the execution of each step help her interpretation and accent her characterisation. She not only tells us how to prepare and practise the steps, but she finds vivid similes for the effect they should make. Thus: "Just a wink of the leg" for an abominably difficult and laborious exercise which should nevertheless be made to give just that effect. Or "a quick *pas de bourrée* must be like three beats of a drum." Indeed she can find drama in even a *pas de bourrée*.

Nothing can be more inanimate than a text-book on ballet technique— except when written by Madame Karsavina. Her chapters on Lost Steps have a poignancy which touches the heart. The quick references to some of her teachers: "This was a panacea of Maestro Cecchetti"; or the maxims of Madame Eugenie Sokolova, carry us in a flash of imagination into their class-rooms. Throughout, her lively mind adds little touches which give the book all the vitality of a ballet performance. Were it not so unusual for a woman who has reached the utmost perfection in one art to achieve complete mastery of another, we would not be so surprised at the manifestation in writing of that great artistry which, although no longer burning on the stage as a Thamar or a Sylphide, still illuminates her everyday life. That the two should be so opposed, the art of words and the art of expression without the hindrance of words, only makes her feat more remarkable, but then— Madame Karsavina is a very rare artist. She has found the way to translate her balletic wisdom into prose.

MARGOT FONTEYN IN " LES SYLPHIDES "

CONTENTS

These essays, which were first published in *The Dancing Times*, have now been completely revised and in part re-written. I am most grateful to the Editors of *The Dancing Times*, Philip J. S. Richardson, O.B.E., A. H. Franks and Mary Clarke, not only for their permission to reprint the articles but for their help and encouragement at every stage. My grateful thanks are due also to Svetlana Beriosova and Prudence Hyman for posing for Paul Wilson's excellent photographs, and above all to Dame Margot Fonteyn for her Foreword to this book.

T. K.

I

❧ INTRODUCTION: SLOWLY BUT SURELY ❧

WHAT I offer here to the attention of the teaching profession as
well as for students is not a setting up of a new method, nor
is it a panacea for all ills, but simply the results of my own experience.
What profited me seems likely to be of some benefit to others, always
assuming that these others are of a normal build. Any malformation
of body, however slight, calls for special methods suitable to the case.

In writing this I kept in mind a child endowed with the physique
of a potential dancer, a child not younger than eight or nine years old.
It is my firm belief that the strain, unavoidable in the strict training of
a professional dancer, must be spared to the very young. I have
watched quite a number of children below the age of eight coming
under the denomination of "child prodigies," and have come to the
conclusion that the premature development of muscles arrests the
normal growth.

We teachers know that the effect of professional training is cumu-
lative—therefore slow. Does it mean that the more promising
children should be kept back to keep pace with the less gifted ones?
I am afraid the answer, at least in one sense, is in the affirmative, dull
as it may seem. It is not enough to obtain a correct execution of a
step; the correctness of it must be firmly consolidated. It must cease
to be a conscious effort but should become an instinct. Psychologi-
cally, however, it is inadvisable to make a child feel it is kept back.
This discouraging thought can easily and profitably be spared to the
child by providing different combinations in the range of such steps
that have to be consolidated before the next degree of difficulty is
attempted.

Therefore our basic principles in teaching should be "slow but
sure." The other fundamental rule is to set the gradual stages of
work in their right order.

I can hear your objection, "Has not the syllabus compiled by the
Royal Academy of Dancing given us the right order?" The syllabus
did so. It has also provided the corner-stone of technical develop-

ment; the two primary aims—the correct placing and the sufficient turn *en dehors*.

But no syllabus can take into consideration the various degrees of aptitude, while a teacher has to deal in one and the same class with more and with less capable children. Some devices have to be thought out for children of lesser aptitude.

The need of such devices is often felt at the elementary examinations. How often we see that a correct *barre* work is not always followed by the same level of execution in the centre.

This can only mean one thing. When the support of the *barre* is withdrawn, the strength of the child is not adequate to achieve the *en dehors* turn in the centre while preserving the correct placing. So it is only logical to say that the strengthening of the muscles is the first on the agenda of professional training. This strengthening work should be gradual, avoiding any over-stress. In other words, the practice must be so planned as to exercise the various muscles alternately. For instance: if, after a *développé* we give the *grands battements* we are putting too big a strain on the same set of muscles—the thighs. On the other hand, if exercises with *pliés* follow on each other, they may possibly overtire the knees. In setting the order of exercises one should keep in mind that, in order to get the tension and the relaxation necessary to the muscles, one should alternate the sustained with the loosening work.

This purpose of strengthening the muscles is well served by dissecting any particular exercise into its component parts and practising each part repeatedly till the muscle governing the movement is seen to have its necessary tension.

As one of many instances of "dissection of exercises" let us take a *ronde de jambe à terre en dehors* where so frequently the hip turns in before the working foot passes to the first position, which it should not do. Instead of continuous movement make the pupil hold each of the three main points of the round: *devant, en seconde, en arrière,* and also the first position, seeing that the thigh is properly tense and turned *en dehors*. The holding of tension is the way to strengthen the muscle. When this exercise has reached perfection, give it with a very slight raising of the working foot off the ground. You will notice that it will then call into action the hip muscle, thus serving as a good preparation for *adage*.

In the next chapter I propose to suggest some exercises leading to steady *adage*. I have tried all of these on the dog—in other words, found them of great help in my own work.

Action photograph by Roger Wood
ALICIA MARKOVA AND ANTON DOLIN IN "GISELLE"
Adage can be a beautiful performance

2

❧ *ADAGE* ❧

ADAGE, to be a beautiful performance, needs very strict attention to details. Even the slight imperfections, such as might pass unnoticed in quick steps, become offensive to the eye in a slow movement of *adage*. Stiffened or drooping wrists, bad grouping of fingers, are enough to mar the beauty of line.

It is strenuous for the teacher to correct so many faults as can occur in *adage* when it is in progress and very difficult for the pupil to concentrate her attention at once on several corrections of the same movement. It is far more profitable to set up the preparatory stages of *adage* before it is done as a whole. A clear understanding of what is required for a perfect execution of an *adage* is the first step towards a systematic preparation.

Apart from the turn *en dehors*, which is for all purposes achieved by the set *barre* practice, what we need are: control of the spine, suppleness of the body, correct and expressive arms and readjustment of balance when weight is transferred from one foot to another. Much of the preparatory work for these requirements could be added to *barre* practice.

"*Asseyez vous bien sur vos reins*" was the favourite advice of Madame Eugenie Sokolova—meaning "get a good grip in your lower back." The working up of this grip controlling the spine is well served by *arabesque alongée* at the *barre*. That is where the teacher can correct the pose fundamentally by seeing to it that the weight of the body goes forward enough to make the supporting leg a centre of gravity. Putting the hand on the lower muscles of the spine the teacher can ascertain whether the grip is there. For the suppleness of body all *ports de bras* with the body bending front, back and side, are of great benefit. Especially good for the purpose is the *port de bras* with the foot *dégagé en arrière*, the body bending forward and then arching backward and the same *port de bras* with the *dégagé* slightly raised off the ground.

A special *adage* exercise which I would like to suggest for the strengthening of the thigh is this: hold a *développé*, quickly lower and as quickly bring up the working leg without relaxing the thigh. The drop must be very slight, not more than two or three inches and even less for a small pupil. Just a "wink" of the leg.

As a preparatory exercise for the readjustment of balance the time-honoured *temps lié* in the centre could hardly be bettered. The current mistake, that of putting the *dégagé* foot on the ground first and then transferring the weight to it, is deterrent to the virtue of this exercise. The stepping on the *dégagé* foot must be simultaneous with the transference of weight; the length of the step must be as far as the toe of the working (*dégagé*) foot points. Any shortening of this side step, bringing in of the working foot before the weight is put on it, does away with much of the usefulness of *temps lié*.

Temps lié en l'air and all derivations of it when there is a stepping from one *développé* on to another must be watched for the same mistake; the weight of the body must be transferred from one foot to the other without lowering the *développé*. When correctly executed the *temps lié* teaches the pupil to feel her balance.

BERYL GREY AND JOHN FIELD IN "LE LAC DES CYGNES"

Dynamics of the Dance. Lengthwise *ballon* showing the movement forward expressed through the whole body

3

✣ *ELEVATION STEPS* ✣

FROM force of habit and because I think the term is comprehensive, I will use the word "allegro" in reference to steps and enchaînements. All my masters applied this musical term to the dance. Allegro needs all the strength that *barre* practice and *adage* can give plus elevation. Natural elevation being comparatively rare, we must look for means of developing it. Here, as in every other aspect of ballet training, a study of the particular set of muscles serving as a spring lifting the body off the ground is necessary.

While the muscles of the knee and those of the thigh are very important factors, it is the Achilles tendon that provides the mainspring of elevation. The function of the Achilles tendon is like that of strong elastic, or, better still, let us compare it to a steel spring. It stretches and contracts—the bigger the stretch the stronger becomes the contraction conditioning the push off the ground. The elasticity of the tendon can be worked up through all forms of *demi-plié*, observing that while the knees bend the heels must remain firmly on the ground. *Demi-plié* in first position, giving it four counts, with a slight pause at each count, is one of the best exercises I have tried and can recommend. To get a corrective to the tendency of the average pupil of pushing out the lower back in this *demi-plié* it is better to practise this exercise facing the wall with both hands on the *barre*.

Battement fondu, both *à terre* and with *relevé* on *demi-pointe*, is another invaluable aid to elevation.

The class of Guerdt at the Theatre School of Petersburg was specially devised to develop the elevation. A few exercises in the nature of a mild limbering were given regularly at the end of the class. We went back to the *barre* facing the wall in the first position; then slowly inclined the body on the right side in *demi-plié* on the right foot, the other foot remaining straight; then on the left side in the same way. In this movement the body should incline to the alternate sides as far as the stretch of the tendon and the support of both hands would allow. This exercise must be done slowly and gently; in the case of younger pupils, only under the teacher's supervision.

Another after-class exercise for elevation was to stand at the *barre* at arm's length facing the wall, toes and heels close together in a most unorthodox first position, then, gripping the *barre* with arms outstretched, to bring the whole body forward maintaining the weight on the gradually bending elbows while the legs remain rigidly straight and the heels adhere firmly to the ground. This exercise helps also to stretch the under-knee muscles.

Enchaînements are, of course, the high school of ballet training. The more varied they are the better they develop the potential artistry, the memory and the quick understanding of a pupil, but on no account should the daily routine of the basic steps such as *assemblé, jeté, temps levé*, etc., be omitted. Even an accomplished dancer cannot dispense with them as she cannot skip the *barre* practice.

In order to impart an artistic finish to execution the pupils must be taught to discriminate between the relative values of each step forming an enchaînement. To bring into relief the main points all

A vigorous leap need not look strained when *ballon* and the control of spine muscles are tuned to help

the steps serving as a preparation must not be emphasised, but, on the contrary, subdued. To take a simple instance; a somewhat laborious *glissade* leading to *assemblé porté* produces an anticlimax. A *coupé devant* preparatory to *arabesque posée,* if done too elaborately so as to amount to a *développé*, takes away from the importance and the ultimate effect of the *arabesque*.

4

𝕏 POINT WORK 𝕏

WHILE it would be difficult to better the already existing exercises and methods of point work, as included in the syllabus, it is worth our while to probe into the reasons which prevent some pupils from deriving the full benefit from those exercises. The fact that the formation of feet varies considerably provides the answer. A foot with toes of average length, when the big toe is not disproportionately

An action photograph by Serge Lido

YVETTE CHAUVIRÉ
An example of beautifully sustained poise on point

long, presents no problem. The other formation, toes too long in proportion to the instep, needs more help than the ordinary set of exercises can supply.

In the latter case, the ensuing weakness of the point work has to be counteracted by giving additional strength to the arch. Apart from an extra dose of *battements tendus*, given at the end of the class, some remedial exercises can help. In very bad cases some readjustment of shoes may be necessary. One of the remedial exercises for strengthening the arch is as follows: with toes and heels close together grip the ground with the toes, then propel the foot forward in a shuffling movement without raising it from the ground; do it with alternate feet, effecting a slow move forward.

When the big toe is disproportionately long and is therefore apt to bend inwards in point work, thus tending to enlarge or even dislocate its joint, the shoes worn for point work should be reinforced by a strip of leather glued inside. The length of the strip must fill the space under the arch, and in some cases can be extended forward so as to give support to the big toe.

In advising a reinforcement of the shoe I have not in mind a block shoe. In fact I consider block shoes harmful for the practice, noisy and clumsy on the stage.

A precautionary measure for avoiding any danger to this joint is

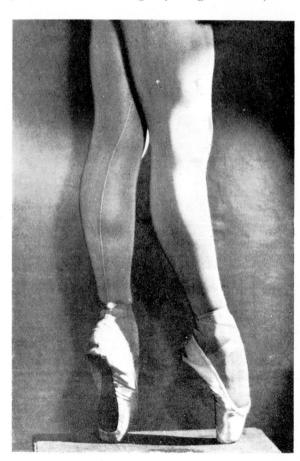

TAMARA
TOUMANOVA'S
LEGS AND FEET

Studio Iris

to have a pad of cotton wool between the big and the second toe. Better still, to use an orthopaedic appliance specially devised, light to wear and not bulky.

In saying that the correct position of the feet when actually on points is not yet the final achievement but that the rising up and coming down must be carefully watched for rolling over, I am only repeating what every teacher says several times a day to the pupils. Nevertheless, it cannot be said too often. Rolling over, especially when the weight of the body comes down, puts a strain on a cartilage of the knee and may even be at the root of this, not unfrequent, injury —slipping the cartilage.

As regards the artistry, the finishing touch of the point work, I would like to draw the teachers' attention to the difference between the sustained movement, holding a pose, and the quick one well termed "*piqué.*" While the sustained movement is generally well understood, I feel that the "*piqué*" so necessary in *pizzicato* movements and in quick *pas de bourrées* is not always as neat and as sharp as it should be. One, two, three, of a quick *pas de bourrée* must be like three beats of a drum and very contained in space so as to avoid an open position on the second count; in other words, it must be well *croisé.* I must again quote my teacher who used to say: "*Brulez vos pas de bourrées.*" The essential difference between the sustained and the *piqué* movement is that the first must be firmly posed and held while the second hardly touches the ground but, so to speak, pricks it.

5

❧ *PIROUETTES* ❧

For those who have no natural aptitude for turning, *pirouettes* are the most difficult of steps. Firstly, because a quick movement is not easy to control, secondly on account of nervousness. But if careful preparatory work is done before *pirouettes* are attempted they become easy and unfailing, the nervousness automatically ceases.

As in every group of steps so in *pirouettes*, only more so, every section of the movement should be checked on separately.

Taking the basic *pirouette* first, and preferably *en dehors* from fourth position, let us see in what order to start so as to verify each contributing factor.

B

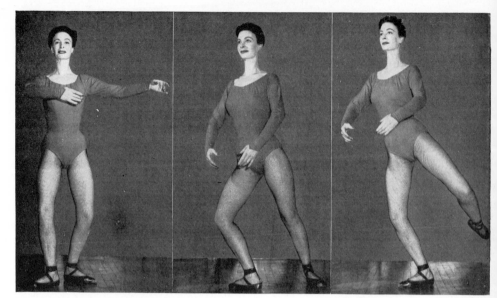

Paul Wilson

A PRELIMINARY EXERCISE TO IMPROVE PIROUETTES

Prudence Hyman posed for the photographs, which show: *left:* weight evenly distributed between both feet (count 1); *centre:* weight transferred to the front foot with both feet firmly on the floor (count 2); *right:* back foot lifted in small attitude and held (count 3, 4). This exercise is intended to be done in the *croisé* position, but it was found that in the taking of photographs the two last movements were better illustrated in the *effacé* position

Preparation is obviously the beginning, there are many details in it and not a single one must be overlooked. When the fourth position is taken the *demi-plié* must relax the knees and the thighs, the heels firmly adhering to the ground, the whole weight of the body pressing down. Next, the hips must be square to the position of the feet. The tendency, very frequent, of throwing out the hip of the working foot (the one that is to be raised off the ground) must be checked. The shoulders have to be, at this stage, in line with the hips. The forearm should be well crossed, the curve of the wrist directly opposite to the shoulder (right wrist—left shoulder, and vice versa), and the other arm open in a straight line with the shoulder and on the level with it. The shoulder-blades must be locked, a grip on their muscles being essential.

Before the actual *pirouette* is done both shoulders should sway slightly in *croisé* position to square again with the hips when the spin begins. The arms should not in this sway move out of their alignment to the shoulders. Certain latitude, however, may be allowed on this point. Some dancers find it useful to let the open arm swing slightly behind the shoulder before the spin. But whether in line with the shoulder or a fraction behind it the elbow of the open arm must on no account drop. If it does drop, then it will pull the weight on one side. Altogether it is most important that both elbows are slightly lifted up and rounded to bring them on a level with the wrists. Now—the weight of the body pressing down, the hips, shoulders and arms set in the right position, the shoulder-blades tightened, we must see that the muscles of the spine are not relaxed.

The distribution of weight comes next. We take it as a rule that the weight must be distributed between both feet, reposing slightly more on the supporting front foot. But this rule does not apply equally to all builds of body; it is the teacher's discernment that should determine the exact distribution of weight. To know how the weight should be distributed in any individual case it is useful to make the pupil take the preparation, then raise slightly the back foot off the ground while remaining in *demi-plié* on the front foot. If the position thus can be sustained this means the distribution is correct.

Relevé is the next stage. It must be practised without turn first: preparation, *relevé*, holding on *demi-pointe* as when *pirouetting* with arms in their final position (at the point between *bras bas* and first position—that is, slightly lower than the chest). In this exercise the point to watch is the heel. It must not shift, nor must it rise off the ground, as it so often does, before the *relevé* has reached its culminating point. When execution of the preparation and *relevé* is correct, an enchaînement, first simple then composite but still without turn, can be set.

For instance: a *pas de bourrée* finishing in preparation in fourth position, *relevé* on the front foot, the working foot coming *sur le cou-de-pied devant, coupé derrière* (on the front foot) and so on, moving across or diagonally. Next this enchaînement could be done with *pirouettes*. It is advisable to set it in four figures: three singles, the fourth double *pirouette*. At this stage of training for *pirouettes* the work of the head must begin.

As we know, the head should turn a fraction of a second after the spin has started and be facing the audience a fraction of a second in advance of the end of the spin. In other words, the head should be left behind at first and then anticipate the end of the *pirouette* at the end.

It is most important to watch that the head is being poised straight on the neck; the slightest incline of it, whether towards the shoulder or forward, destroys the visual sense of balance. Directly controlling the visual sense of balance are the eyes, a seemingly small detail often

not thought of. The eyes must steadily fix an imaginary point ahead, they should not wander or look at the ground. For this purpose exercises in the centre such as *assemblé soutenu en tournant, détournés* and similar movements are very helpful. They train the head to remain over the left shoulder (if moving from left to right) in the first half-turn and to come over the right shoulder in the second half-turn, and this is good for both the head and the eyes.

ANTON DOLIN
Weight brought over the front leg in big 4th position should serve as preparation for *pirouettes en dedans*

6

❧ *PIROUETTES — Continued* ❧

BESIDES the technique and the strength necessary to *pirouettes* there is another factor in this step more difficult to control than some possible technical faults—the nervousness. Dancers with a perfect all-round technique may have some bad spells when they seem to have lost their *pirouettes*. Fear, not unlike the fear of heights natural to some people, may be the reason for it, or else some former mishap, like a fall on a slippery floor while *pirouetting*, may have unsettled a dancer for a long time. The apprehension before this step often makes the dancer anticipate the moment of taking off: she starts spinning before she has established her balance. This nervousness also prevents the necessary relaxation of muscles preparatory to the tension of the *relevé*.

The best way to deal with the temporary loss of *pirouettes* is to stop doing them for a time and meanwhile dissect the whole movement into its component parts, checking on each till it is perfect and comes naturally. A dancer, if continually performing, cannot of course even temporarily eliminate the *pirouettes* if they are the integral part of her dance. She should, however, during her class work, persist in re-establishing her balance and her best way to do so is to include more *relevés* in the side and centre practice.

A good way towards regaining one's balance is to do a small *échappé sauté* and a quick *relevé* on one foot, the other foot coming on the *sur le cou-de-pied*. The *échappé* must have the necessary relaxation on touching the ground. This was a panacea of Maestro Cecchetti when dealing with faulty *pirouettes*: he compared the movement to the action of a ball springing straight up off the ground.

But in the case of pupils the fear of *pirouettes* need never arise if two principles are observed in teaching: one, never to let the pupil attempt spinning before she is ready for it, and the other to perfect every section of a *pirouette* in a separate exercise.

The preparation in the small fourth for the girls and in the second position for the boys is the easiest for the basic teaching of *pirouettes*. The ultimate perfection of a dancer, though, is to be able to spin from any position such as the fifth, the running *pas de bourrée* in the first, or from a *relevé* on one foot and even from an *arabesque fondue*. This variety of *pirouettes* is seldom used now, but they should with advantage be practised in the advanced class, as they afford more variety.

For the advanced pupils and for the dancers who want to vary their steps I would like to recall a very effective enchaînement of *grandes pirouettes à la seconde* as done in the old version of *Don Quixote*. It started upstage coming down diagonally and went thus: starting with a *dégagé* behind in *croisé pas de bourrée* over *en tournant, renversé en attitude sauté, pas de bourrée* under finishing the half-turn of the *renversé*, quick *fondu* on the front foot as for *pirouette en dedans*, two *pirouettes en dedans à la seconde*. Another good enchaînement of *pirouettes* with disguised preparation is a *pas de bourrée couru* in first position, quick *fondu* on both feet in fifth, two *pirouettes en dehors*. This enchaînement with four *relevés passés* following the *pirouette* was used in the variation of the ballet *Le Reveil de Flore.*

At present the *grande pirouette à la seconde* seems to be a step reserved for male dancers. In the old ballet it was often used in enchaînements for a ballerina. It is not too difficult when done with *pas de bourrée en tournant* and *renversé*, as both these steps gather an impetus, helping the *grande pirouette.*

As a rule the *pirouettes* that avoid an obvious preparation are the most effective: they give an impression of ease, though in themselves may be more difficult. An enchaînement with double *pirouettes en dehors* from an *arabesque fondue*, in the ballet *Le Corsair,* may, I hope, tempt dancers to try it. In the tempo of 2—4 it took four bars to one enchaînement. It went like this: *pas de bourrée en tournant* over, pass the working leg from the *sur le cou-de-pied* into *arabesque fondue croisée* (one, two); *arabesque fondue sautée en tournant* making two rounds (three, four, five, six); deeper *fondu* on the count six, double *pirouette en dehors* from *arabesque*, arms *en couronne* (seven). Finish the *pirouettes* in *sur le cou-de-pied devant* (eight). Recommence the enchaînement, this time without *pas de bourrée* but bringing your leg from *sur le cou-de-pied*

into *arabesque croisée* by a movement like a *ronde de jambe à terre* slightly raised. This enchaînement repeated four times should be done on one spot, like *fouettés*, in the centre of the stage.

Prudence Hyman demonstrates the end of *renversé en tournant*

Paul Wilson

7

❧ *TENSION AND RELAXATION* ❧

To correct a fairly current mistake of the students in thinking that the push off for spinning a *pirouette* comes from the feet only, it is necessary to make them realise that in itself a *pirouette* is a composite movement: a simultaneous push upwards and a spin. The function of the feet in a *pirouette*, after establishing the balance, is to raise the body straight up on the points. That is why the *relevés* from a *fondu* preparation from fourth or second position on to the *demi-pointe* or *pointe* of one foot are so useful. They teach one to find down and up balance. The spin comes from the shoulders and the arms. The swing of the shoulders from *croisé* or rather over-crossed position to square eventually with the hips gives its real impetus to the spin. The arms, also following the same swing as the shoulders, give an additional help. That it is the swing of the shoulders that gives the main impetus has been well demonstrated by some Italian ballerinas, Brianza and Legnani, for instance, who often did their *pirouettes* with arms crossed over the chest or arms laid on the hips (last act of *Coppélia* and other ballets of rustic character). In such instances they had only the swing of the shoulders to set them spinning.

In itself an easy movement, needing no great strain, the action of the shoulders before a *pirouette* seems to be a difficult one for most pupils to grasp. There can be but one explanation for it: the lack of mobility in the upper part of the body. A certain amount of stiffness is a besetting sin of present-day training. A properly trained torso should be supple as well as strong; this is an essential condition of poise and ba'ance as well as of elegance of line. Théophile Gautier, while praising the supple and graceful torso of Fanny Elssler, remarks of other dancers that they are no more than "a pair of frenzied legs under an immovable torso."

The aim of our exercises, as far as the technique is concerned, is to make the legs capable of moving freely round their axis—the hip. Much the same principle should govern the training of the torso; it should be able to move without pulling the whole of the body with it. To achieve this it is necessary in the early stages of training to inculcate upon the mind of the pupil the importance of *épaulements*; first the elementary ones and subsequently the quick changes of *épaulement* in steps and enchaînements. For example, *sissonnes sautées* over in marked *épaulement effacée* to the right, same to the left, done in a moderately quick tempo will be useful to the purpose. Or else the same *sissonne* over in *épaulement croisée*. In the progressive stage of training the exercises for the torso need to be more strenuous and include bending forward, arching backward and rotatory movements. There were two kinds of exercises practised daily in my time: at the *barre* and in the centre.

Holding on to the *barre* in a *développé devant*, not too high, the body folds forward to the leg and then bends back, still maintaining the *développé*. The same bending forward and backward was done while maintaining an attitude. That most academical teacher, Madame Anna Johannsen, used to say at the end of the class: "Now do your twists." That was an unconventional *port de bras* in the centre. Toes and heels close together, the torso bent low forward so as to reach the toes with the hands, then arched back, the arms doing a full *port de bras*—to the sides, down and up, *en couronne*. Still in the same position of heels and toes with arms *en couronne*, the torso was turned right and left as far as it could go, taking care not to displace the hips; the head turned over the shoulder to look back right and left. Next there was the rotatory movement of the torso: down to one side, back, and to the other side, the figure thus traced a full circle of the upper body over the immovable hips.

It is well to bear in mind that in all turns and half-turns the rigidity of arms at the wrong moment stops the spin or the swing instead of helping it. The time to tense the arms is when they close in the final position. They must not be strained in the preparation. The same rule applies to the thighs and the knees, they should relax in *fondu* preparation and tauten in the *relevé*.

A *fouetté* on the point from *éffacé devant* into an *attitude ouvert* offers a good instance of the timing of tension and relaxation of the arms. Doing it from right to left (on the left foot) it starts with the working leg raised *devant*, the right arm at the side (shoulder level), the left crossed in *demi-bras*. Now, if the left arm is stiffened before it opens to the side, it will impede the turn. The left arm should swing freely to the side, the wrist leading. Once in the open position the left arm must tense itself to hold the attitude.

Not only in turns but in all steps the tension and the relaxation of muscles must be well-timed with the movement.

VIOLETTA ELVIN AND JOHN HART IN "HOMAGE TO THE QUEEN"

A properly trained torso is supple as well as strong

8

❧ *SUMMARY* ❧

In this chapter I want to underline the main idea behind the early chapters of this book: why the professional training, especially the elementary one, must be slow, gradual and adapted to each individual build. Chiefly because if the initial mistakes have not been eliminated in the early stages they may become engrained in the pupil and will be difficult, sometimes impossible, to eradicate later on. Grace, vitality, vigour can at times disguise faults, but the scope of an imperfect dancer is limited and further progress arrested. Only a technique, the foundation of which has been built step by step, can give perfect mastery of the art.

Preparing the ground for faultless execution is a slow, painstaking task of the teacher. For, to point out the mistake to a child or a young student is not enough—with the best will in the world the young may not know how to do better; it is the teacher only who can spot the cause of the mistake and find the remedy. Therefore the mere repetition of the same step in its entirety does not answer the purpose; a faulty step should be, so to speak, analytically dissected and an exercise given to that particular set of muscles which does not work correctly. Thus, laying the foundation of sound technique, the work must take time. The training must be a sustained effort, but on no account must it be forced. Some obstinate fault may be due either to lack of attention or to lack of strength or else to a physical shortcoming. To each of these cases must be applied a different method of correction. While the lack of strength can be remedied by devising exercises which give help to the weaker muscles, backwardness and lack of attention need a psychological approach. In fact, the insight into a pupil's psychology is essential to a teacher. No less essential is the capacity to find out the cause of an obstinate fault. If the fault is due to a physical shortcoming, the repeated remarks "not to," etc., will only exasperate the pupil and will not bring an improvement. Let us take a concrete case, that of insufficient stretching power of the under-knee muscles. It would be beyond the pupil's power to tauten the knees unless she is helped in getting rid of ther defect which prevents her from tautening them. This particular defect and other similar ones, all due to stiffness of muscles rather than to any physical malformation, yield to mild limbering—such as I have suggested in previous articles.

Summarising the views I have given on the training of a classical dancer, I would like to draw the attention of my readers to the fact that the perfect technique of a classical dancer is becoming rare at present. The decline of it is manifest in ballets of Romantic style, such as *Giselle* and *Les Sylphides*. Though following the choreographic design fairly accurately, the steps are not what the choreographer intended them to be. They are transposed from an elevated sphere to the *terre à terre* execution. The *ballon* and the preservation of a pose when landing are seldom seen. The great and beautiful feature of Romantic style such as landing from a *fouetté en l'air* into a long-sustained *arabesque fondue* is practically a lost art. What is the cause of the decline from perfect seemingly effortless elevation? The answer is easy: the omission of exercises needed for *ballon*. The mainspring of elevation and of the smooth controlled landing is the Achilles tendon and the strength of the knees. If their muscles have not received proper attention in the elementary stages of the dancer's training, there can be no perfect *ballon*. To put it into practical terms —*battements fondus* and all the forms of *demi-plié* with pressure on the heel should figure largely in daily practice; a quick flexing of the knees alone without pressure on the heels does not serve the purpose. Let *battements fondus* be the "daily dozen" of practice and they will develop a *ballon* necessary to a classical dancer.

THE ENCHAÎNEMENT IN ITS ATTENUATED FORM

A photograph taken during an actual performance of the beginning of the enchaînement referred to below.
Here it is seen in its attenuated form in the Mad Scene.   Giselle is Margot Fonteyn

9

❧ *LOST STEPS* 1 ❧

FOR a long time I have been worried about "lost steps."   So many
ingenious and some highly technical enchaînements of the old ballets
never occur at the present time.   I am especially referring to the
classical ballets of the early and mid-nineteenth century.   Toward the
1850's the simple, charming choreographic tradition accepted the
virtuosity of the Italian school, on condition that any *tours de force*
should seem effortless.   The elevation, vertical and horizontal,
remained a basic quality of this enlarged technical scope.   So much
so that the repertoire of *terre à terre* ballerinas was limited to a few
ballets.

I cannot believe that the steps and the manner of execution of the old classical ballet, were they but known, could be unacceptable to the present-day taste. The success of the Danish Ballet confirms me in my opinion.

If the naïve choreography of Bournonville charms the eyes and the senses in virtue of the purity and grace of movement, of the clarity of its dramatic purpose, how could the same qualities enhanced by an effortless virtuosity fail to please? It is the purpose of these chapters to draw attention to that unused wealth of steps that made the fabric of the old ballets.

The peak of virtuosity within the bounds of classical form has been reached in *Le Corsair*—the technical difficulties of this post-Romantic ballet are on the level of those of *The Sleeping Beauty* but needing far greater elevation. The earlier and simpler choreography (though by no means an easy one) of a purely Romantic *Giselle* is constantly before our eyes.

The fairly accurate revival of Coralli's masterpiece, well done as it is, yet has lost much of its original style. It took me some time to puzzle out why the same choreography, the same set of steps, are not the same any more in their effect and in tieir emotional value. It is because the choreography of *Giselle* has been transposed into another key. Originally composed for a dancer of exceptional lightness, it was in my time reserved for ballerinas with more than average elevation. This seems to be no longer so. Bringing *Giselle* down to the level of any technically accomplished dancer meant a sacrifice of its sublime feature, its spiritualised lightness. *Giselle* does not easily adapt itself to the means of a *terre à terre* dancer. In order to make such an adaptation many rhythms have to be quickened. And so, beginning with the waltz in the first act, the steps of the *haute envolée* seem shrunk, as if half done. There seems to be a lack of perception of the style of Romantic ballet for this waltz to be treated as a *demi-caractére* piece. The Romantic and the post-Romantic tradition highly "balletised" any dance with a character flavour as long as it was rendered in the ballet medium—toe dancing.

All through the waltz the ballerina's main enchaînement, *ballonné pas de basque*, when done in the quickened tempo, is no more than a *ballonné pas de basque*. In the original version it looked more than a simple enchaînement such as any pupil could execute. Taken, as it used to be, in slower tempo, interpreted in accordance with the original intention of the choreographer, this simple enchaînement partook of a peculiar virtuosity. Difficult as it is to explain any movement in

words, I will attempt to give an idea of what effect this main enchaînement of the waltz was meant to produce. To begin with, the initial
position for the start had a very marked *épaulement croisée*. With the
body and the head softly but definitely inclined towards the supporting
foot, the *ballonnés* were done in a forward movement, very low, the
working foot as if caressing the ground, the instep flexible. The
strong (first) beat of the *pas de basque* was a step of high elevation.
The level of its rise off the ground was enhanced by the crossing of
one leg over the other while in the air, as if suspending the final soft
développé en avant of the *pas de basque*. The change to a marked *épaulement croisée* on the other side occurred during the high level of the
pas de basque.

Further still from its classical tradition is the *ballotté* in the first
act. It needs a slower tempo for the proper crossing and folding of
both legs in the air on the highest point of elevation. It should pause
in the air with both legs crossed, both knees bent.

The instances of steps that answer to their name but lack the
compass of the classical tradition are more numerous in the second
act. If not entirely "lost" they have strayed into the by-paths of
classicism. I am convinced that the way to bring back the now rare
quality of *ballon* would be through a well-devised practice.

Lightness and height of jump are also helped by a good *développé*
and there is a set of exercises which used to be practised under the
direction of Johannsen, which consists of the following movements.
First, sitting on a chair placed close to the wall, execute a slight *plié*
in second position with hands resting on knees; then gradually the
body slips off the chair until it is only propped against it, going down
as low as possible. The second exercise is, still on the chair, to hold
the heel when pointing the toes in a *développé en avant*. Then to lead
from that position to *développé à la seconde*. During the second and
third movements one should be sitting firmly on the chair. This
exercise is not for young pupils.

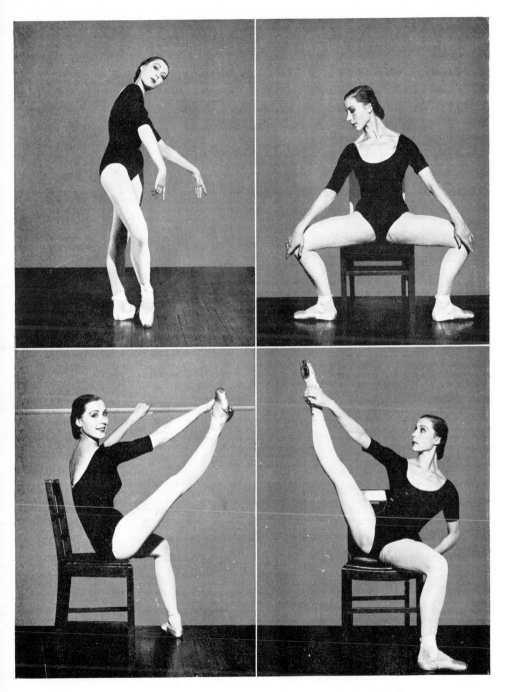

Top Left: Épaulement for *ballonné* in the first enchaînement of the Waltz, Act I of *Giselle*
Top right, bottom left, bottom right: 1st, 2nd and 3rd movements of limbering exercises on a chair, by Christian Johannsen

These photographs, and those on page 33 by Paul Wilson, were posed for by Svetlana Beriosova.

❧ *LOST STEPS* 2 ❧

THE second act of *Giselle* deals with the supernatural element so much used and so inspiredly expressed by the choreography of the Romantic period. This element was suggested mainly through etherealised dancing and helped by stage effects, not in use any more. The technical requirements for the part of *Giselle* in the second act are a high and effortless elevation, the breadth of horizontal leaps and, not the least, the capacity of alighting from a high jump into a long sustained *arabesque fondue*. Essential, too, are the marked *épaulements* and a special distribution of balance in the *développés* on the points which precede the elevation steps very often. To illustrate a concrete example of those various points of technique I will dissect the first dance of *Giselle* in the second act; it is when Loys kneels down, covering his face. The first enchaînement of the dance would read thus: *jeté fondu* to the right foot, *développé* in the second position on the point of the right foot, *chassé, fouetté en tournant en l'air* finishing in *arabesque fondue*. As done now, this enchaînement is a somewhat restricted version of the original one: all the steps being of equal calibre and therefore of diminished effect. The intention of the choreographer was to have high lights, emphasis on certain steps, as well as the breadth of movement. Thus the *jeté* (without rise) had a considerable stretch (*étendue*) to the right, bringing the body, arms and head, softly inclined, to the same side. In a more picturesque description it might be said: the body describes a curve reaching sideways over the central column of support. The *développé* on the point preserves the curve of the body and is held not for one beat only, but one-and. *Chassés* should be travelled considerably to the left in a soft gliding movement so as not to impair the emphasis of the enchaînement—the *fouetté en l'air*; this last is a big elevation step coming down in *arabesque fondue*, which is held on the beat four. This *arabesque fondue* is not a sudden drop, but a graduated *plié*, so that at its last moment it is lower than at its beginning.

In general, there was much importance attached to definite *épaule-*

Top left: Épaulement for *jeté* at the beginning of the enchaînement of the 2nd Act of *Giselle* (1st movement).
Top right: Épaulement for the *développé* of the enchaînement (2nd movement). *Bottom left:* Alighting in *arabesque* in the enchaînement after the *fouetté en l'air*. *Bottom right:* One of the typical poses of the Romantic ballet.

ments in the old ballets. The *fouetté en l'air* in *arabesque* without turning, also in the second act, presented to the eye the profile of the body, the following *fouetté en l'air en tournant* has therefore a full turn and so gained in effect. This enchaînement occurs frequently in the second act of *Giselle*. It can be said that the Romantic ballet sought an elongated line, it used the foreshortened one (*raccourci*) but seldom.

There is, in particular, one step in the second act of *Giselle* which, given its full scope, looks like a swift flight through the air. It is only a *pas de chat jeté* in diagonal, but it used to rouse the whole audience to spontaneous applause. Beginning at the top of the stage by the last wing, it finished at the first wing downstage. Low at first, it gained impetus and height as the *jeté* got more extended in length and the come-down between became shorter and shorter. To gain the full effect this step must have a fraction of what, for the want of a better word, might be called staying up in the air. In other words, in alighting it only touches the ground to push off but does not stay down. Is this a magic trick? Positively not. Supple tendons, controlled breath, extension of the *jeté* and well-timed effort and relaxation will produce the desired effect. In the present version this step is not carried to its logical conclusion—the last *jeté* finishing behind the wing so as to create the impression of the dancer soaring away and disappearing. The *déboulés* in the present version of this step pulls up its impetus. Incidentally, *déboulés* as an inevitable finish of a diagonal movement, was hardly, if ever, used in Romantic choreography. Looking back on the training in my time, I can say positively that no teacher was as successful in devising exercises for *ballon* as Pavel Guerdt. There was not a single pupil in his class who fell short of lightness of jump. He varied his enchaînements, but one item never varied. The elevation steps always began by the small sharp *changements de pieds* for thorough "warming" of the instep. Every class finished in the same way, with the difference that, after sixteen *grands changements de pieds* with a deep *fondu* came the small ones. Towards the end the push off the ground had to be vigorous, quick and sharp, and the rise off the ground higher. In this way the wise teacher provided the means for two kinds of jumps: a soft and a sharp push off. When practising in the evenings by ourselves we used to have competitions in *changements de pieds*, going as far as hundreds.

II

❧ *THE USE OF THE INSTEP* ❧

It was said of Emma Livry that she rose without effort and alighted softly and gracefully. It seems significant that the critics contemporary to the great dancers of the classical school of the Second Empire should have used this word "alight" for the coming down after an elevation step. "To land" has crept into use since. Though the two may denote the same action there is a world of difference between them. There are so few dancers who do alight nowadays that one is anxious to bring to light the reasons for the paucity of these precious qualities—lightness and softness. Block shoes may be partly responsible for the harsh landing, but the main reason for it is the lack of elasticity in the foot itself and the wrong use of the instep.

The functions of the foot are to lift the body off the ground in elevation steps or *relevés* and to minimise the impact of its weight when coming in touch with the floor.

If the upward rise is worked in a movement starting from the heel and passing through the metatarsus to the toe, thus using every muscle of the sole, the whole strength of the foot contributes then to the elevation. The incorrect use of the sole of the foot may be particularly noticeable in a series of *relevés* in *arabesque* on points, the step out of the waltz in *Les Sylphides*. If the foot works only partially and not through the whole of the sole, the *relevés* become jerky, the leg raised in *arabesque* goes up and down because it lacks the full support of the working foot to sustain its weight at its proper level.

In alighting the same process as in taking off is reversed. The first contact of the foot descending on the ground should be through the high *demi-pointe,* then the under instep is brought down before finally the heel is lowered. The correct work of the instep must be established at the very beginning in the elementary side practice. A very slow *battement tendu* in the daily practice will prove infinitely more to the purpose than any spoken correction during the elevation steps. That is, if the leading out of the *dégagé* is done through the whole of the foot. It must be watched that the heel does not leave

the ground before the toe reaches the ultimate limit of the *dégagé*.
Then only the instep arches to point the toe and the heel rises.   When
closing the *dégagé* the foot comes down gradually through the whole
of the sole, the heel must be brought firmly on the ground in closed
position.   A very important point is to tighten the muscles only in
pointing the toe and to relax them when the heel is down in position;
the want of relaxation is a common fault amongst pupils when doing
battements tendus.   This lack of relaxation after the tension may lead
to what is called "muscle-bound" condition.   The slow rising up on
demi-pointe and the slow coming down into position is an excellent
exercise for the foot.   Further, a slow lowering down from *demi-pointe*
into a *fondu en arabesque* will greatly contribute to the elasticity and
the strength of the instep.   No less important is it to insist on the
toes being fully arched in the elevation steps.

There is a variation from an old ballet which could not be ade-
quately performed unless the feet had the elasticity and the sensitive-
ness equalling those of our hands, the variation of the golden fish in
the *Little Hunchbacked Horse*.

Set to the tempo of 6—8 this variation began with a small *coupé*
under and five *ballonnés penchés*, extensively travelled.   This was
followed by six *arabesques ouvertes fondues*, also travelled, so that the
whole length of the stage from the last wing on the right (from the
audience) down to the first wing on the left was covered by the
dancer with the enchaînement repeated three times.   Both the *ballonnés*
and the *arabesques fondues* move along with the same motion of the supporting foot as that of a soft *relevé* on *demi-pointe*; they do not rise off
the ground and are meant to suggest a swimming movement.   The
travelling of the step is achieved by the supporting foot propelling
forward towards the extension of the *ballonné*.   This form of *ballonné*
is called "*penché*" because the body throughout leans forward and
sideways towards the working leg.   Altogether there used to be a
greater variety of *ballonnés* in the old ballets than now.

An action photograph by Anthony

ALAN CARTER (CENTRE) WITH JUNE BRAE AND MICHAEL SOMES IN
"HARLEQUIN IN THE STREET"

Elevation helped by the full use of the instep

12

BATTERIE

Two chief factors of a good *batterie* are the perfect turning out of the thighs and a good elevation. While, at the risk of sounding unorthodox, I hold that an excessive turning out of the working leg in *adage* is not altogether advisable as it is apt to put too much strain on the hip of the supporting leg, there is in my opinion not such a thing as being too much turned *en dehors* in beats. The first condition of the vertical *entrechat* is that in passing out and in, it must be restricted in compass. This stands for quickness and brilliancy. The vertical *entrechat* must start from and finish in a perfect fifth position.

The opening of the legs, while in elevation, should be sideways, not forwards and backwards. This step may be compared to elevated *battement tendu* in the second, with both legs working simultaneously but more restricted as to the scope of *dégagé* than the *battement tendu*. So it follows logically that the work on *batterie* can only start when the pupil can close her feet in a perfect fifth.

In my schooldays when having the evening practice under the supervision of a senior girl we were made to face the wall and, holding on to the *barre* with both hands, hold the fifth position for quite a time pulling in the lower back. This seems to me as good a foundation of *batterie* as can be.

Another exercise for *batterie* was this: from the fifth position the working (front) leg opened to the second, off the ground but not raised, stretching only as far as to be just open off the first position the toe not pointed; it then closed behind in the fifth and repeated the movement from behind to the front. In fact, it was the ground pattern of an *entrechat quatre,* the four sections of the movement to be done in one count. The more advanced form of this exercise was the ground pattern of an *entrechat six* with precisely the same motion as in the previous exercise. The next stage would be to rise on the *demi-pointe* of the supporting foot while passing the working foot in and out and to come into the closed fifth with a slight *fondu* on both feet, this time the toe pointed.

There are two schools of thought regarding the practice for and the execution of an *entrechat*. The one school considers the *battement sur le cou-de-pied* as an exercise for beats, the other takes as a foundation for it the *battement tendu*. In the first case one leg is very slightly relaxed in the knee while beating, thus doing an attenuated *battement sur le cou-du-pied* in the air. The other method, which I think a better one, is to have both legs straight, the thigh muscles tensed while executing the beats. The second method has the advantage of giving more strength to the push off the ground: both legs contributing equally to the jump.

As in other elevation steps two kinds of technique in rising off the ground should be cultivated for *batterie*: the soft and the quick *plié*. As an example one might take the *changements de pieds* as usually done at the end of a class. Slow at first with strength derived mostly from the knees and afterwards the quick ones pushing up mainly from the feet and the tendons, with no more than a relaxation of the knees in between. The quick push off the ground facilitates *entrechats* and makes them more effective. Often, though, the slower taking off from a good *plié* is necessary if the rhythm of the music and the set of an enchaînement demand it.   To try and make the difference clear here are two instances of *entrechat-six* enchaînements.   The first one, set to a sharply defined rhythm of 3—4 (perhaps *rubato*), might be this: beginning with the right foot in front an *entrechat-six* from a *temps de cou-de-pied, arabesque ouverte à deux bras sauté* on the *pointe* and slightly travelled forward.   The preparative *temps de cou-de-pied* and the *entrechat-six* both are done on the "and" before the beat, the *entrechat* closes down on beat one, the *arabesque sautée* on the *pointe* holds for two beats.   This enchaînement done with alternate feet and travelling in a straight line from up to down stage, if repeated for 12 or 16 bars, is very effective.   It was used in *Sylvia*.   This is for a quick push off.

For a slow rise from a deeper *plié* the enchaînement from *Raymonda* may serve as an instance.   The count is 6—8.   It begins at the top right corner of the stage (from the audience) and travels diagonally down; the *épaulement croisée* is preserved throughout.   It goes like this: *développé* in second on the point left leg (one, two, three), arms *en couronne*; *entrechat-six* taking its preparation from the close down of the *développé* into the fifth position *devant* (four, five, six), arms coming down in *bras bas*.   As we have here three beats allowed to *entrechat* it shows that the *plié* before and after should be such as in a *grand changement de pieds* and not in the nature of a push off.

The music of the variation into which Petipa introduced this rather strenuous combination can be found in the piano score of *Raymonda*, Variation 2, on page 93.   This enchaînement takes the 12 last bars and finishes with a *coupé* under and *posé* in *arabesque à terre* on the final chords.

❧ BATTERIE — *Continued* ❧

In the preceding chapter I discussed only the vertical *batterie*. In travelled steps such as *brisés* and certain kind of *cabrioles* the neatness of the beat and the lightness of the motion depend in great measure on the placing of the body. How often one says to a pupil: "Take your weight with you in the line of your travelling. Don't leave it behind." It means that in *brisés* the body must be slightly inclined towards the working foot when the foot is in *dégagé*. The weight so distributed propels the motion forward and achieves neat landing. Leaving the weight behind, that is, entirely on the supporting foot, always gives an impression of lameness: the actual closing of the *brisé* won't then land on both feet simultaneously, there will always be a split second between the feet closing in the fifth.

It is always a good thing to practise *brisé* first at the *barre*, in slow motion. Facing the *barre* do *dégagé* behind on count one, with rather a deeper *fondu* on the supporting foot than it would be in the actual elevation step; rise in *relevé* from *fondu* on the half point of the supporting foot, beat over with the working foot and close behind in *fondu* on count two. Though the travelling of the *brisé* cannot be effected, in this *barre* exercise, the incline of the body can be easily corrected. Altogether, many of the elevation steps are improved when thus practised with a *relevé* at the *barre* because the *relevé* from *fondu*, used in such exercises, works up the strength of the muscles used in elevation, those of the tendon and calf.

I remember a very charming *coda* for a male dancer. Travelling from up to down stage diagonally every step of the four counts is a small quick beat. It begins with the right foot behind in the *épaulement effacée* (left shoulder); *jeté battu devant* with the same *épaulement* (one); *cabriole devant* with the left foot (two); *cabriole fouetté en tournant* finishing in *croisé* (right shoulder) (three); *jeté battu dessus* coming into the original position of *épaulement effacée* (left shoulder) (four). It looks brilliant if done to a quick measure and travelled diagonally. This repeated sequence of small beats is equally suitable for a woman.

In *batterie* of higher elevation, such as a *glissade* behind and *cabriole devant*, the effect of elevation is better achieved if the accent of this step is put on the finish of the *cabriole* instead of at the beginning. This needs explaining. A *cabriole devant*, as it is most often done in *épaulement effacée*, must preserve the same line of body as that of a *développé* in the same *épaulement* in *adage*: the body leaning slightly back over the supporting foot. To preserve this line of the body while up in the air it is essential that the *dégagé* in the air of the working foot should not be a high one. As we know, the first condition of a good *cabriole* is that the supporting foot comes up to beat against the working foot, not vice versa. What happens if the *dégagé* is done on too high a level? The supporting foot must also come high to beat under, it is impossible then to prevent the body folding forward in a hairpin fashion. The actual beat, therefore, must be only moderately high, the highest point of the step is when the working foot opens in a high *dégagé* after the beat.

On the other hand, when it comes to a *cabriole derrière* either from a *posé* or a *pas de bourrée couru*, the incline of the body is well forward of the supporting leg, only slightly less so than in the arabesque of an adage. An absolute turn *en dehors* of the feet, especially of the supporting one, in this *cabriole* is more necessary than in any other step. Without the good turn *en dehors* the beat cannot be done by the calves, it happens then on the shin bone. This is dangerous as well as unsightly.

A good lead up to a correct *cabriole derrière* is to include an enchaînement in the elevation steps in a somewhat slower tempo. *Posé* with the foot well turned, two *temps levés sautés* in *arabesque, pas de bourrée dessous* and recommence moving diagonally forward. It should be strictly insisted that the leg *en arabesque* position, while in *temps levé sauté*, maintains its level and does not go up and down. The jump in *temps levé* then will depend entirely on the elevation of the supporting foot. This is also a good strengthening exercise for all kinds of elevation steps.

To this I must add that, though in this *cabriole* the body leans forward over the supporting leg, the spine must be strongly arched to prevent a heavy landing and to preserve the curve of the body as it should be when the rise in the air has to suggest the forward as well as the upward movement.

An action photograph by Lipnitski

SERGE GOLOVINE AND KATHLEEN GORHAM IN "L'ANGE GRIS"

This step illustrates the main points of *cabriole derrière*, body forward of the supporting leg, back arched, the calves meeting in a correct position

14

❧ SUBORDINATE STEPS ❧

OVER and above the mere technical precision of steps there is the manner of expression, the phrasing of the dance. It is closely wedded to the musical phrasing but it also has its specific laws because of the dynamic quality of the dancing—traversing of space. Phrasing of the dance sequence means putting accent where it is needed and subduing the small links between the accentuated movements. Unless the dancer keeps this in mind the sequence of steps becomes very like an unpunctuated sentence.

As regards dynamics, too much stress put on subordinate steps diminishes the impetus. This point can be easily explained by taking as an instance a sequence of *glissade, grand jeté en avant ouverte* either around the stage or moving cross-ways.

Clearly the step to be accentuated here is the *grand jeté en avant*, not the *glissade*. When, as it often happens, the dancer puts an equal, stress on both steps, he not only misses the right accent but also wastes his strength on the *terre à terre* movement while the strength should be conserved for the high jump. This mistake occurs if the *glissade*, instead of quickly closing in the forward push, remains open longer than it should; if, instead of gliding forward, the *glissade* remains for a time suspended in open position. In itself this *glissade* should be inconspicuous to make the *grand jeté* emphasised. If it is not so, the step will look laborious, besides actually hampering the next movement. But more than that: the back leg remaining open longer than it should and, so to speak, dragging along in a strained slow motion pulls the weight of the body back while the whole body should be propelled forward to help the oblique elevation of the *jeté*. All elevation steps in lengthwise motion reach their perfection only if the movement forward is continuous and unhalted. And so it will be in the given sequence if the *glissade* comes through without halting, closes quickly, allowing time for the *coupé fondu* preceding the *grand jeté*. The *coupé fondu* it is that gives the jump its height, the *glissade* is only the means of moving forward.

There are the slow soft *glissades* of *adage*, the *glissades* leading to jumps and the quick "*glissades pressées*" that had been much in use in the 18th century.

The *glissade* of *adage* allows of the pause in the second *dégagé* on the condition that the first *dégagé* (stepping out) is done from a *fondu* position and that the second one closes also in *fondu*.

The *glissades* leading to jumps, whether done through the fourth or through the fifth position, need not stop in closing but only go through the position. The most important point in these *glissades* is to make sure that the body follows the direction towards the stepping out *dégagé*. Only then could the slight jerk backward, attendant on the wrong distribution of weight, be avoided. In my schooldays *glissade* was first taught in slow motion: *dégagé*, step out on half point, hold on the half point with the other foot in *dégagé*, close in *fondu*. Usually it was done across in one direction with a change of *épaulement*. In this way it was easy to see that the weight was placed correctly on the stepping out foot because, if it was not, the second *dégagé* could not be held. When this elementary form of *glissade* had been mastered, the movement was done quickly without holding on the half point, but only stepping on and closing down.

For the *"glissade pressée"* the set enchaînement was: *glissade* forward, *glissade* back (both in *épaulement croisée*), *glissade de côté devant* (same *épaulement croisée*), *glissade de côté derrière* (*épaulement croisée* of the other shoulder). This enchaînement was done in a quick tempo stepping on half point, but not holding on.

Another, often misused subordinate step, is *coupé*. Let us take the instance when it precedes a *posé*. It is a current mistake, especially in *adage*, to do the *coupé* as high as if it were a *développé*. To step from it into a *posé* either in attitude or in arabesque one needs to bring the leg down again. In my opinion this would disturb the flowing grace of *adage*; the time not being enough to hold a sustained *développé*, such movement would be more in the nature of kick than either of a *coupé* or of a *développé*. But if the subordinate steps such as *glissade* and *coupé* have to be toned down and be not prominent at the expense of the stronger, accented movement, they should nevertheless have the utmost precision and accuracy.

To sum up what I have said about discrimination between the main and the subordinate steps, I could not do better than quote these words out of an 18th-century treatise on art. Speaking of a great actor, Dorat says: "From a deliberate omission of small details he drew strength to render brilliant the chief features of his part; he used in his acting a delicate shading which increased the value of it and finally brought out his masterstroke, always obtained at the price of some sacrifice."

15

❧ BALANCE ❧

BALANCE, as applied to dancing, is the faculty of adjusting the weight of different parts of the body so as to enable a dancer to maintain equilibrium with the minimum of support, as on the extremity of a highly arched toe. Without a perfect sense of balance a dancer cannot sustain the pose on her *pointe* long enough to impress it on the memory of the spectators; nor can the execution remain strictly rhythmical if the come-down from a pose anticipates the music, as it happens if the balance is off-centre.

The perfect balance can be acquired only after years of training when the strength of the legs and of the spinal muscles has become adequate to sustain the weight distributed fore and aft of the supporting leg. But the foundation of balance must be laid from the very beginning and start with the right stance at the *barre*—in other words, the initial placing is of the greatest importance. The very first step towards it is to ascertain that the point of support in the arm holding on to the *barre* is between the wrist and the elbow, on no account must support be derived from the shoulder. Next it must be carefully watched that the *dégagés* and the *développés* do not displace the centre of gravity, which rests on the supporting leg. *Dégagés* must open only as far as it is consistent with the weight of the body remaining entirely on the supporting leg. The tendency to lead the working foot further out in *dégagé* than it should go can easily be corrected if, for instance, an exercise is given of a slow *dégagé* in a second, slow raising of the foot off the ground, not high, and taking the supporting arm off the *barre*. A frequent mistake in *battement tendu glissé* is to throw up the *degagé* too high. Besides bringing the torso into commotion, the high throw of *battement tendu glissé* does not serve the purpose of this exercise: the purpose being to enable the feet to pass in and out of a closed position swiftly and within a small compass. We have only to think of the quick *échappés* on the points or an *entrechat-six* to realise that they derive their precision directly from the *battement tendu glissé* and that, unless the speed needed for these steps is prepared by the

46

MARGOT FONTEYN
This pose shows a beautiful adjustment of vertical balance

glissé exercise, the *échappes* and the *entrechats* will stop short of brilliancy.

In the case of beginners the correct stance at the *barre* is often endangered by their efforts to throw up the leg too high in *grands battements*. The working up of the upward stretch of the legs must be gradual and only allowed the full height when the thigh has acquired a sufficient turn *en dehors*. Before this stage is reached the excessive

47

zeal of the pupil in *grands battements* results in her pulling the supporting leg away from the upright position and in turning the working
thigh *en dedans*.

When the initial work for the foundation of balance—the correct
placing and the turn *en dehors*—has been consolidated, it would be
beneficial to include some special exercises for balance into the side
practice. Here are a few suggestions:

(1) *Développé en avant*. Place the front foot from the *développé* on
the ground as far as the toe points, the heel well turned *en dehors*.
Transfer the whole weight of the body on the front leg in *fondu*, the
upper part of the body well forward over the front leg as in an *arabesque alongée*. Remain in this position while counting one-two. Step
on the back leg, re-transferring your weight and resuming the original
position of *développé devant*. This second movement is held with the
leg up *en avant* for two counts. The second part of this exercise—
stepping on the back leg—needs a strong contraction of the spinal
muscles and pulling in of the working hip.

(2) Hold on to the *barre* facing the wall in fifth position. *Demi-
plié*, extend the front foot to the side, still in *demi-plié*, keeping your
weight well on the supporting leg. Step to the side on the *demi-pointe*
of the extended foot bringing the supporting foot in *coupé sur le cou-
de-pied en avant*. Repeat several times with alternate feet, transferring
the weight from one foot to the other, taking care to step on the extended foot as far as the toe points.

(3) Facing the wall, *temps de coup-de-pied* (*soussus* on half point) in a
well-closed fifth position. Remaining on *demi-pointe* bring the front
foot in a *coupé devant* in *sur le cou-de-pied* and disengage it to the side, let
go of the *barre*. Remain in this position as long as you can, then close
in fifth behind, ready to repeat the exercise on the other foot. When
this exercise is done with the extension of the foot, either front or
back, it need not face the wall, but is better done in the usual position,
holding on to the *barre* with one hand.